R.L. STINE

graphix PRESENTS:

Goosebumps

SLAPPY'S TALES OF HORROR

Adapted and illustrated by Dave Roman, Jamie Tolagson, Gabriel Hernandez, and Ted Naifeh

Color by Jose Garibaldi

The Goosebumps series created by Parachute Press, Inc.

Based on *A Shocker on Shock Street* © 1995 Scholastic Inc., *The Werewolf of Fever Swamp* © 1993 Scholastic Inc., *Ghost Beach* © 1994 Scholastic Inc., and *Night of the Living Dummy* © 1993 Scholastic Inc.

Library of Congress control number: 2014959511

ISBN 978-0-545-83600-5 (hardcover)
ISBN 978-0-545-83595-4 (paperback)

10 9 8 7 6 5 4 3 2 1 15 16 17 18 19

Printed in China 38
First edition, September 2015

Edited by Adam Rau and Sheila Keenan
Color by Jose Garibaldi
Book design by Phil Falco
Creative Director: David Saylor

HELLO, SLAVES!

You're probably wondering
why I've brought you here.
It's not for anything *pleasant*,
I can assure you.
Well, it's pleasant for me,
because I get to see you
tremble with dread.

HA-HA-HA!

I've prepared four spine-tingling tales of horror
to fuel your nightmares!
Now, you may think you can look away,
you may think you can escape, but you *can't*.
All you can do is try to make it to the end
of this book without going ***mad*** from ***fear***!

Our first story,
A SHOCKER ON SHOCK STREET,
is a happy little tale of terror and mayhem set in
a not-so-amusing amusement park. Prepare yourself
for the ride of your life... or death!

HA-HA-HA-HA!!!

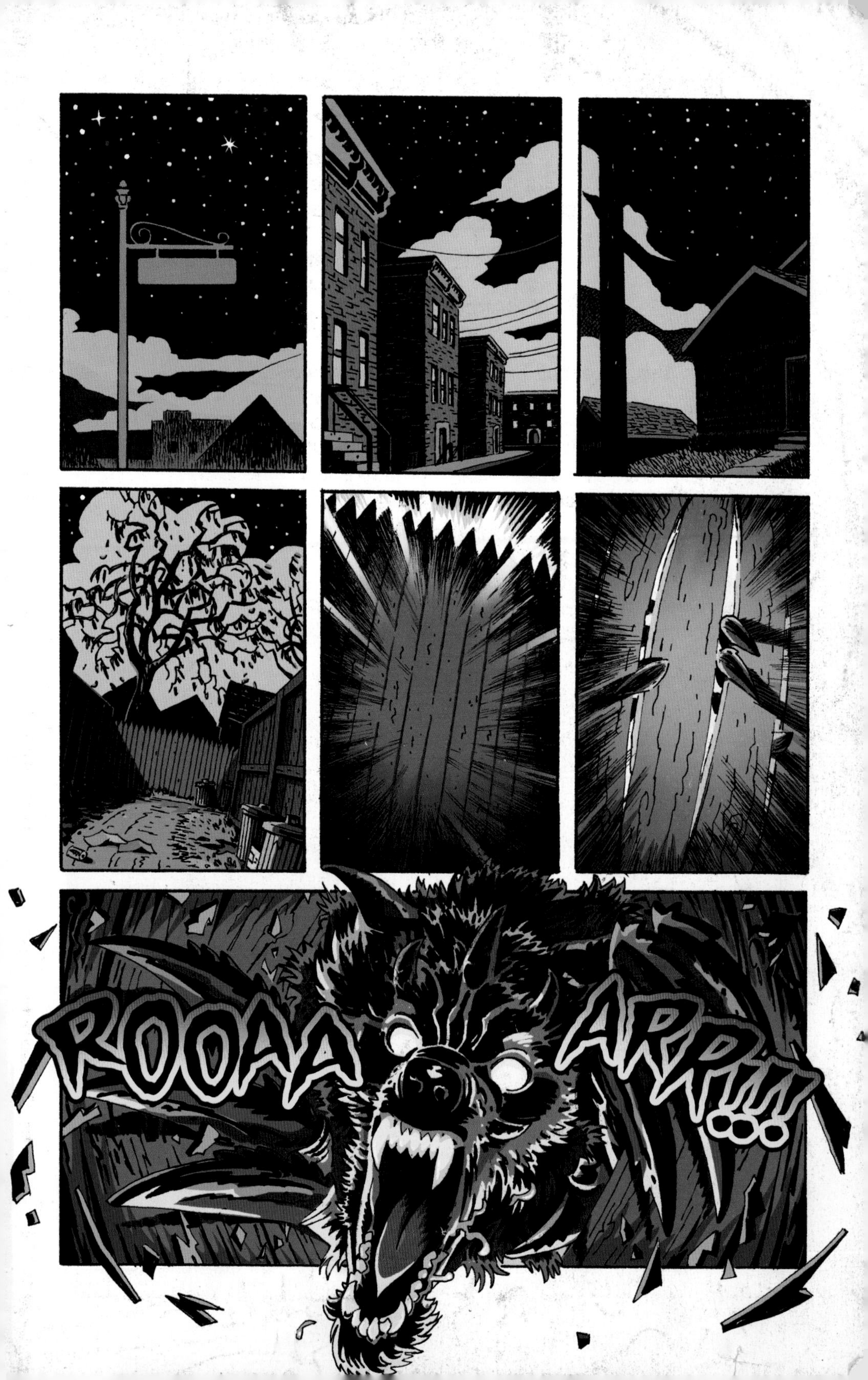
ROOAARR!!!...

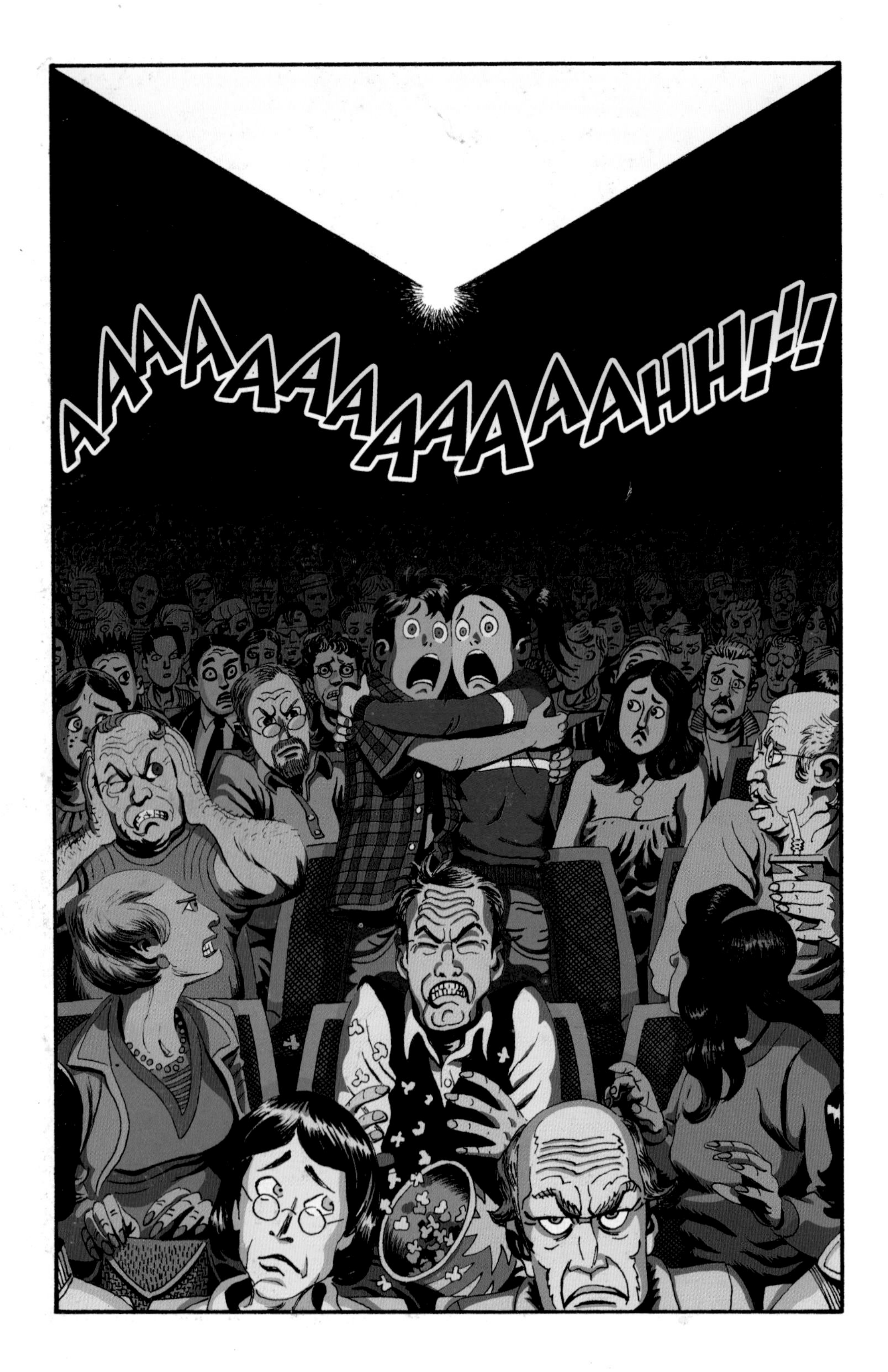
AAAAAAAAAAAAHH!!!

I CAN'T SEE THE SCREEN.
SHHH!!!

WHAT'S YOUR PROBLEM, ERIN? IT'S ONLY A MOVIE.
YOU SCREAMED TOO, JOSH!

SHHH!!!
SHHHHH!!!

BLAM
BLAM
BLAM
BLAM

The End
a Shocker Studios Production
CLAP!
CLAP!
CLAP!
CLAP!
CLAP!

GREAT SPECIAL EFFECTS!
GREAT SPECIAL EFFECTS? I THOUGHT IT WAS ALL REAL!
HA-HAHA!
PRETTY GOOD MOVIE.
HUH? PRETTY GOOD?
IT WASN'T SCARY ENOUGH. SHOCKER V WAS WAS A LOT SCARIER.
YOU SCREAMED YOUR HEAD OFF!
I ONLY DID THAT BECAUSE I SAW HOW SCARED YOU WERE.
YOU JUMPED OUT OF YOUR SEAT. YOU GRABBED MY ARM AND—
LOOK OUT! YOU TWINS SHOULD BE MORE CAREFUL.
WE'RE NOT TWINS!
WE'RE NOT EVEN BROTHER AND SISTER.
WE'RE JUST FRIENDS.
YOU KNOW THE COOLEST THING ABOUT THIS MOVIE?
NO. WHAT?
THAT WE'RE THE FIRST KIDS IN THE WORLD TO SEE IT!
GOOD THING MY DAD WORKS WITH A LOT OF MOVIE PEOPLE...
SLAP!
...SO HE COULD GET TICKETS TO THIS SNEAK PREVIEW.
YOU KNOW WHAT ELSE WAS REALLY COOL? THE MONSTERS!
THEY DIDN'T LOOK LIKE SPECIAL EFFECTS AT ALL.

HMMPH! I THOUGHT THE ELECTRIC EEL WOMAN LOOKED LIKE A BIG WORM.
THEN WHY DID YOU JUMP WHEN SHE SHOT A BOLT OF ELECTRICITY?
I DIDN'T JUMP. YOU DID!
DID NOT! YOU JUMPED BECAUSE IT LOOKED SO REAL!
HEY— WHAT IF THEY'RE ALL REAL MONSTERS?
DON'T BE DUMB.
AAAAAAAAAHHHH!
ROAR!
SORRY IF I SCARED YOU!
LET'S GO UPSTAIRS AND SEE MY DAD.
YOUR DAD HAS A REALLY COOL JOB. BUILDING THEME PARKS AND DESIGNING RIDES? COOL!
YEAH. MY DAD IS AN ENGINEERING GENIUS. I THINK HE IS THE WORLD EXPERT ON ROBOTS. HIS ROBOTS WILL DO ANYTHING! HE USES THEM IN HIS PARKS AND MOVIE STUDIO TOURS.

DAD!
MONSTER WORLD
OH, HI, YOU TWO.
CHECK THIS OUT. DO YOU KNOW WHAT THIS IS?
SOME KIND OF TRAIN CAR?
IT'S A TRAMCAR. GUESS WHERE THIS TRAMCAR WILL BE USED...

...IT WILL BE USED AT THE *SHOCKER STUDIO TOUR.*
YOU'VE BEEN WORKING ON THE TOUR FOR FOUR YEARS. IS IT FINALLY GOING TO OPEN?

YES. BUT BEFORE IT DOES, I WANT YOU TWO TO TEST IT OUT.

YOU MEAN IT?
YES! YES! YES!

DAD, THE *SHOCK STREET* MOVIES ARE THE *BEST!* AWESOME! IS IT SCARY?

THE *REAL* SHOCK STREET? YOU GET TO RIDE DOWN THE REAL STREET WHERE THEY MAKE THE MOVIES?

YES. THE REAL SHOCK STREET, AND I WANT YOU TO GO BY YOURSELVES. I THINK THAT WILL MAKE IT MORE EXCITING FOR YOU.

IT'S SO GLOOMY OUT.
PERFECT FOR A HORROR MOVIE TOUR.
WHICH MONSTERS ARE WE GOING TO SEE?
I'M NOT TELLING YOU.
I JUST WANTED TO WARN ERIN. SHE MIGHT FAINT.
I'M WARNING YOU!
SHOCKER
STUDIOS
BEWARE
BEWARE
WE'RE HERE. TAKE IT EASY, GUYS!

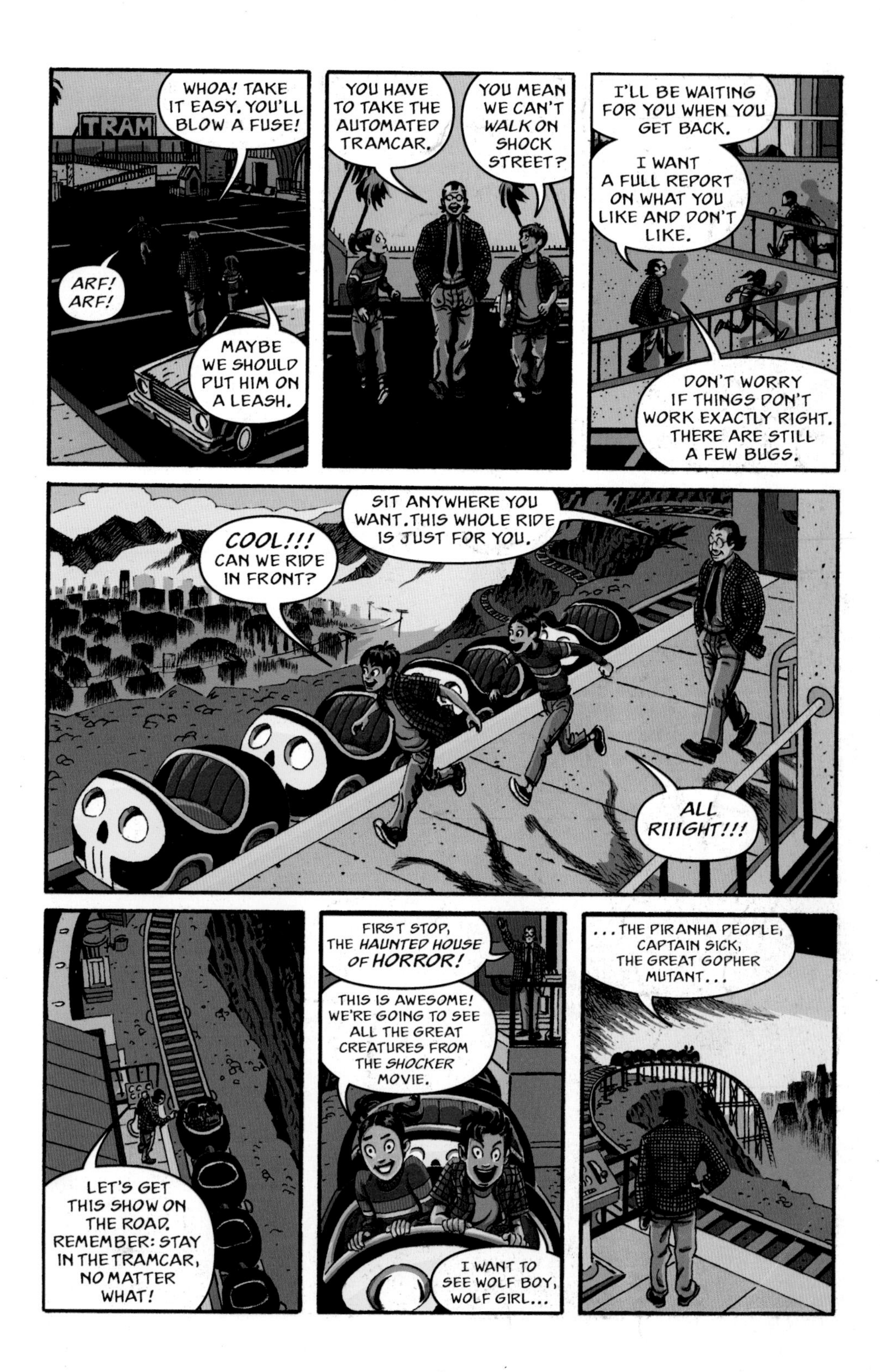
TRAM
WHOA! TAKE IT EASY. YOU'LL BLOW A FUSE!
ARF! ARF!
MAYBE WE SHOULD PUT HIM ON A LEASH.
YOU HAVE TO TAKE THE AUTOMATED TRAMCAR.
YOU MEAN WE CAN'T WALK ON SHOCK STREET?
I'LL BE WAITING FOR YOU WHEN YOU GET BACK.
I WANT A FULL REPORT ON WHAT YOU LIKE AND DON'T LIKE.
DON'T WORRY IF THINGS DON'T WORK EXACTLY RIGHT. THERE ARE STILL A FEW BUGS.
COOL!!! CAN WE RIDE IN FRONT?
SIT ANYWHERE YOU WANT. THIS WHOLE RIDE IS JUST FOR YOU.
ALL RIIIGHT!!!
LET'S GET THIS SHOW ON THE ROAD. REMEMBER: STAY IN THE TRAMCAR, NO MATTER WHAT!
FIRST STOP, THE HAUNTED HOUSE OF HORROR!
THIS IS AWESOME! WE'RE GOING TO SEE ALL THE GREAT CREATURES FROM THE SHOCKER MOVIE.
I WANT TO SEE WOLF BOY, WOLF GIRL...
...THE PIRANHA PEOPLE, CAPTAIN SICK, THE GREAT GOPHER MUTANT...

AAAAAHHHHHHHHHHH!
KEEP
WHOOOOOOOOSH

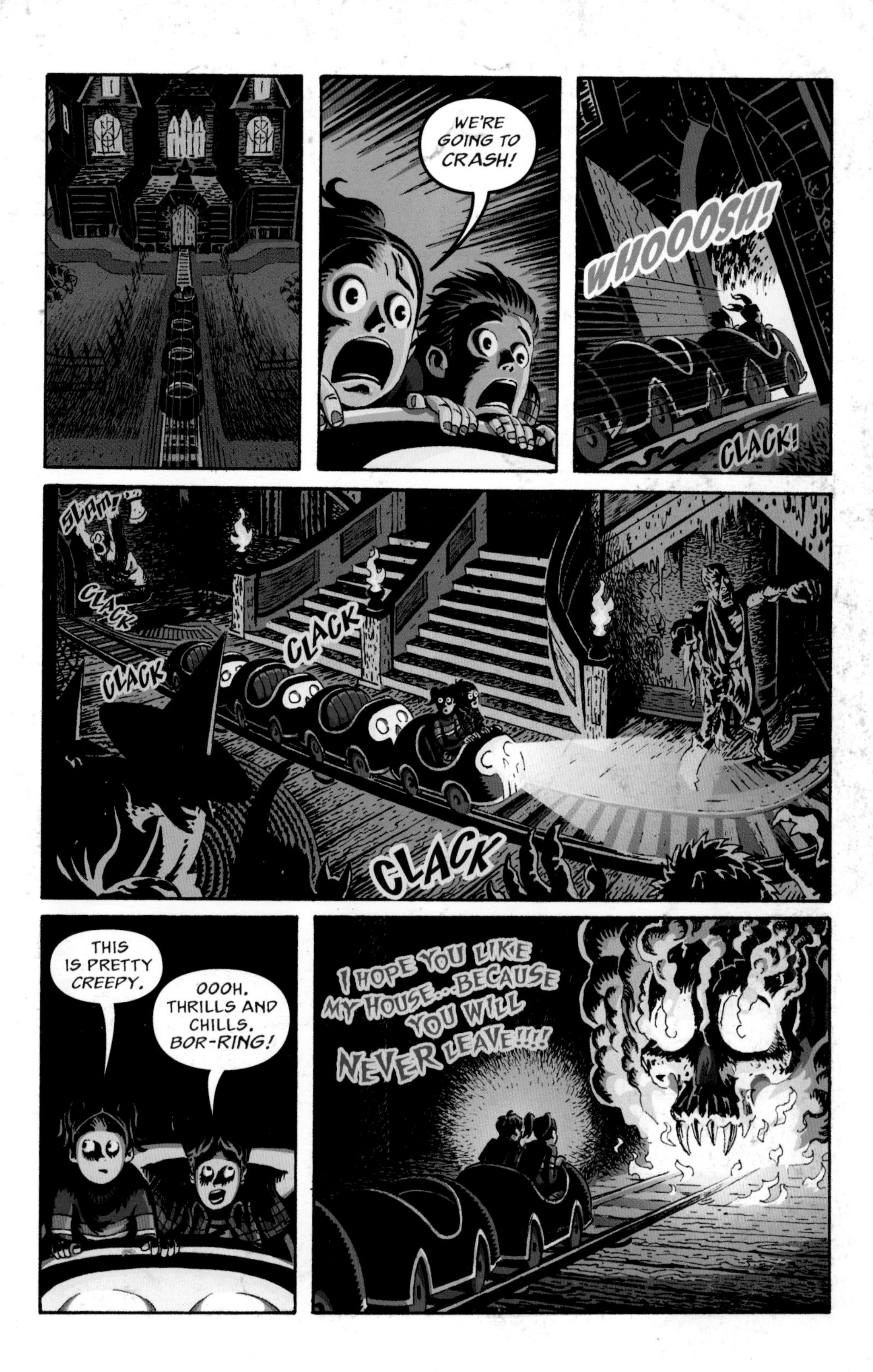
WE'RE GOING TO CRASH!
WHOOOSH!
CLACK!
SLAM!
CLACK
CLACK
CLACK
CLACK
THIS IS PRETTY CREEPY.
OOOH. THRILLS AND CHILLS. BOR-RING!
I HOPE YOU LIKE MY HOUSE...BECAUSE YOU WILL NEVER LEAVE!!!!

HA! HA! HA! HA! HA! HA!

AAAAAAAAAAAA
AAAAAAAAAAA
AAAAAAAAAAAA
CLACK
CLACK
CLACK-I-TY
CLACK
WHOA! THAT WAS EXCELLENT!
I'M GOING TO TELL YOUR DAD THAT ROLLERCOASTER RIDE WAS THE BEST!
Y-YEAH. I-IT WAS KIND OF FUN...AND SCARY.
HEY. WHERE ARE WE?
THERE'S NOTHING AROUND HERE. WHY DID WE STOP?
JOSH...
THERE'S SOMEONE THERE!

GRRRRRRR!
SNARL
L-LEAVE US ALONE!
WOOOOOOOOOOULD YOU LIKE AN AUTOGRAPH?
HUH????
WANT A PHOTO? THIS IS THE AUTOGRAPHING PART OF THE TOUR.
HEY! YOU'RE APE FACE!
TOXIC WILD MAN!
SWEET SUE!
THE TOADINATOR!

WHEN I SAW THEM CREEPING OUT, I THOUGHT I'D HAVE A COW!
IT'S JUST A BUNCH OF ACTORS IN COSTUMES.
BUT THEY LOOKED SO REAL. THE TOADINATOR'S HANDS WERE REALLY SLIMY. APE FACE'S FUR WAS SO REAL.
THE MASKS WERE AWESOME. HOW DO THEY GET INTO THOSE COSTUMES? I DIDN'T SEE ANY BUTTONS OR ZIPPERS!
THEY'RE MOVIE COSTUMES, SO THEY'RE BETTER THAN REGULAR COSTUMES.
BEWARE
PLEASE REMAIN IN THE CAR AT ALL TIMES.
YOUR NEXT STOP WILL BE THE CAVE OF THE LIVING CREEPS!!!!
THINK THERE ARE BATS IN THERE?
BATS ARE UGLY AND DISGUSTING. I HATE THEM.
LOOK OVER THERE! A VAMPIRE BAT!
HUH? WHERE?
HA! HA! HA! HA! HA! HA! HA!
YOU'RE NOT FUNNY.

OHHHH.
PLOP
WEIRD! I'VE NEVER SEEN A WORM THAT BIG.
PLOP
I-IT DROPPED FROM THE CEILING. IT'S ICE-COLD.
PLOP
PLOP
I-I-I I GOT ONE, TOO!
YUCK!
PLOP
PLOP
PLOP
PLOP
PLOP
PLOP
PLOP
PLOP
PLOP
PLOP
PLOP
PLOP
PLOP
PLOP
OHHH! HELP!
PLOP
YEOWWWWW!
PLOP
PLOP
PLOP
PLOP
PLOP
PLOP
PLOP
THEY STOP-P-P-ED FALLING.

THAT WAS TOTALLY GROSS! DO YOU THINK THOSE DISGUSTING WHITE WORMS WERE ALIVE?
OF COURSE NOT. THEY WERE ROBOTS OR SOMETHING.
I'M NOT SURE. THE WAY THEY WRIGGLED AROUND–
EVERYTHING HERE IS FAKE. JUST ASK YOUR FATHER.
I'M NOT SO SURE...
WHY DID WE STOP HERE? IT'S JUST A BIG EMPTY CAVE.
SNEEZE!
HEY! CAN ANYBODY HEAR US?
DRIP
DRIP
DRIP
DRIP
I THINK THIS TRAM IS STUCK OR SOMETHING.
PLUNK
PLUNK
YOU MEAN WE'RE STRANDED HERE?
PLUNK
WE CAN FIND A WAY OUT.
BUT WE'RE NOT SUPPOSED TO LEAVE THE TRAM. GET BACK IN. IF IT SHOULD START UP...
I THINK IT BROKE DOWN.
YOU'D BETTER CLIMB DOWN. WE HAVE TO WALK.
DRIP
WALK? IN THIS CREEPY, DARK CAVE? NO WAY, JOSH!
PLUNK
DRIP
PLUNK
DRIP
DRIP
PLUNK

I'M GOING TO WALK. ARE YOU COMING WITH ME, ERIN?
UH... UH... UH...
DRIP
DRIP
DRIP

BEHIND YOU!
WHOA!!!
CHITTER
CLICK
WHAT IS THAT THING?
IT'S A– PRAYING MANTIS!
HA-HA! OF COURSE! WHY SHOULD WE BE SCARED? IT'S A BIG ROBOT.
HUH? BUT, JOSH.
IT ISN'T REAL. IT'S PROGRAMMED TO WALK UP TO THE TRAM. IT'S ALL ON A COMPUTER.
IT'S...UH... REALLY LIFELIKE.
CHITTER
YOUR DAD IS A GENIUS AT THIS STUFF!
HE SAID THERE WERE STILL SOME BUGS. HA-HA-HA! GREAT-LOOKING ROBOTS!
SCREEE
DRIP
CLACK
DRIP
DRIP
DRIP

CLICK
THEY MOVE SO SMOOTHLY, YOU CAN'T EVEN TELL THEY'RE MACHINES.
WE BETTER GET BACK TO THE TRAM.
CHITTER
DRIP
DRIP
CLICK
IT'LL PROBABLY START UP AGAIN NOW THAT WE'VE SEEN THESE GIANT BUGS.
HISSSSSSS!
HEY! IT WON'T LET US PASS!
WE--WE'RE SURROUNDED!
MAYBE THEY'RE VOICE-CONTROLLED.
STOP!
STOP!!!
SPLAK!
YUCK!
WATCH OUT! THAT BLACK STUFF IS LIKE HOT GLUE!
OWW!
HOW DO YOU NORMALLY GET RID OF BUGS? YOU STEP ON THEM!
BUT, ERIN, THEY'RE BIG ENOUGH TO STEP ON US!

SKREEEEEE
SKREEEE
IT'S WORTH A TRY!
STOMP!
STOMP!
LET'S GO!
CHITTER
CLICK
I SEE AN OPENING IN THE CAVE WALL!
CLACK
CHITTER
CLICK
CLACK
POP!
OOF!
JOSH?
ERIN! HELP! THEY GOT ME! THEY'RE EATING ME!

APRIL FOOLS!
YOU JERK! YOU SCARED ME TO DEATH!
DON'T PLAY ANY MORE DUMB JOKES. THIS PLACE IS TOO SCARY! THOSE BIG INSECTS...
YEAH. THEY WERE SO REAL! HOW DO YOU THINK THEY MADE THEM SPIT LIKE THAT?
HEY, ERIN- LOOK WHERE WE ARE!
WOW! THIS IS REALLY SHOCK STREET... WHERE THEY FILMED ALL THE MOVIES!
IT DOESN'T LOOK THE WAY I IMAGINED...IT LOOKS EVEN SCARIER!
THIS EMPTY LOT IS WHERE THE MAD MANGLER HUNG OUT IN SHOCKER III. HE MANGLED EVERYBODY WHO WALKED BY.
JOSH, COME BACK. IT'S GETTING DARK.
SCARED, ERIN?
NO! IT'S JUST AN EMPTY LOT.
PEOPLE ALWAYS THOUGHT IT WAS AN EMPTY LOT... UNTIL THE MAD MANGLER JUMPED THEM!

I WISH I HAD A CAMERA.
I'D REALLY LIKE A PICTURE OF ME STANDING IN THE MANGLER'S LOT.
...OR EVEN BETTER!
HEY! WAIT UP!
...A PHOTO OF ME STANDING IN THE ACTUAL SET WHERE THEY FILMED CEMETERY ON SHOCK STREET.
LET'S GO, IT'S GETTING LATE.
YOU DIDN'T USED TO BE SUCH A TOTAL WIMP!
I-I JUST HAVE A BAD FEELING ABOUT THIS CEMETERY.
IT'S PART OF THE TOUR.
BUT THE GATE IS CLOSED!
HA HA HA HA HA HA HA HA
JOSH-?
HA HA HA HA HA HA HA
JOSH? WHERE ARE YOU?

HA HA HA
CHECK OUT THESE GRAVES!
BEN DOVER 1812-1872
SID UPP 1912 1975
JIM SOCKS. GET IT?
BEN DOVER. SID UPP.
THESE ARE ALL PRETTY FUNNY. HA! HA! HA!
COOOOOME DOOOOWN!!!
THIS IS SO COOL. THERE MUST BE A SPEAKER HIDDEN IN THE GROUND.
COME DOWN!
COMEDOWNWITHUSSSS!

COME DOWN
HELP! OH, HELP!
YOUR SOCKS AND SNEAKERS! PULL THEM OFF!
COME DOWN WITH USSSS!
HURRY!
SOMETHING IS WRONG!
THE ROBOTS ARE OUT OF CONTROL!
WE'VE GOT TO FIND MY DAD!
WE HAVE TO FIND THE TRAM.
CUT THROUGH HERE!
SPLOTCH
SQUELCH
SPLUSH

COME DOWN COME DOWN COME DOWN WITH US!
THIS MUD IS COLD.
WE RAN INTO A SINKHOLE.
TRY TO GRAB SOMETHING.
THERE'S NOTHING TO GRAB.
YAAAAAA!!!!!
COME DOWN COME DOWN COME DOWN WITH USSSS!
IT'S SUCKING ME DOWN.
I'M SINKING FAST!
JOSH! I'M TRAPPED! THE MUD IS BUBBLING OVER MY NECK!
GLUB
ERIN!
CHOKE!!!!

YANK!
GASP!
AAAAAAAAAAAAAA
OOF!
OW!
THUD!
IT'S WOLF GIRL AND WOLF BOY! YOU SAVED US! THANK YOU!
PLEASE— CAN YOU HELP US GET BACK TO THE TRAM OR THE MAIN BUILDING?

GRRRRRRRRRRRRRRRRRRRRRRRRR!
WE KNOW YOU'RE ACTORS. BUT WE'VE HAD ENOUGH SCARES FOR TODAY. OKAY?
THEY'RE NOT ACTORS. SOMETHING IS TERRIBLY WRONG.
GET UP! MAYBE THEY CAN'T REACH US UP HERE.
RUN!
WE CAN'T OUTRUN THEM.
CLATTER
O'WOOOOOOOOOO!
JOSH! THE TRAM!
RUN!
CLATTER

I-I CAN'T MAKE IT!
RUN! YOU'VE GOT TO!
OOF!
WE'VE GOT TO TELL YOUR DAD THAT THIS PLACE IS MESSED UP!
JOSH— LOOK!
HA HA HA HA HA HA HA HA HA
WE AREN'T THE ONLY PASSENGERS.
HA HA HA HA HA
HOW DID THEY GET ON THIS TRAM?
THE TRAM IS PICKING UP SPEED!
HA HA HA HA HA HA
JOSH, WE'RE GOING THE WRONG WAY.
HA HA HA HA HA HA
WE'VE GOT TO JUMP!
WE CAN'T JUMP, WE'RE GOING TOO FAST!

HA HA HA HA HA HA HA HA
ZZZZZZZAAAAAPPPP!
DID YOU SEE THAT?
I SAW IT, BUT I DON'T BELIEVE IT. HOW DID THE TRAM GO THROUGH THE WALL?
DO YOU THINK THE CASTLE REALLY ISN'T THERE?
THERE'S ONE WAY TO FIND OUT.
IT'S SOLID. IT'S A REAL WALL.

IT'S A GHOST TRAM...A GHOST TRAM FILLED WITH SKELETONS!
BUT WE RODE IN IT!
I'M SICK OF MYSTERIES! I'M SICK OF BEING SCARED!
YOUR FATHER CAN EXPLAIN IT ALL!
I DON'T WANT HIM TO EXPLAIN IT. I JUST WANT TO GET AWAY FROM HERE!
JOSH, LOOK! WE MUST BE HEADING BACK TO THE MAIN PLATFORM! YES!
OH NO.
WE'RE BACK ON SHOCK STREET!
OOOOOOOOOO!
I DON'T WANT TO BE HERE!
RUN!

OOOOOOOOOOOOOOOO

OOOOOOOOOOOOOOOOOOOO
JOSH!
TRIP!
AAAAOOOOOW
WE'RE TRAPPED!
AAAAAAAAAAAAAAAAAAA
...AAAAND CUT!

WHAT'S UP, GUYS?

I'M RUSS DENVER.

GOOD JOB! YOU LOOKED REALLY SCARED.

H-HUH?

WE WERE REALLY SCARED!

I'M SO GLAD TO SEE A REAL LIVE HUMAN!

THE TOUR—IT'S TOTALLY MESSED UP! THE CREATURES... THEY'RE ALIVE! THEY TRIED TO HURT US!
IT WASN'T LIKE A RIDE! IT WAS REALLY GROSS!
WHOA! WHOA!!
IT WAS ALL SPECIAL EFFECTS. DIDN'T THEY EXPLAIN WE WERE FILMING YOUR REACTIONS?
MY DAD DESIGNED THIS STUDIO TOUR. HE DIDN'T TELL US ABOUT ANY MOVIE BEING FILMED.
IT'S OKAY. WE JUST GOT A LITTLE SCARED.
MY DAD MUST BE REALLY WORRIED. CAN YOU TELL US HOW TO GET TO THE MAIN PLATFORM?
NO PROBLEM. GO RIGHT IN THAT DOOR STRAIGHT THROUGH SHOCKRO'S HOUSE OF SHOCKS.
WON'T WE GET SHOCKED WITH 20 MILLION VOLTS OF ELECTRICITY IN THERE, LIKE THE MOVIE?
THE HOUSE IS JUST A SET. IT'S PERFECTLY SAFE. GO OUT THE BACK AND YOU'LL SEE THE MAIN BUILDING.

I'M SORRY FOR YELLING BEFORE. I WAS JUST SO SCARED...
NO PROBLEM.
JOSH! DON'T GO IN THAT HOUSE!!!
JOSH! WAIT! STOP!
NO!
ZZZAAAAAPPP!

NOOOOO!!!
JOSH! JOSH!
WAKE UP, JOSH! SNAP OUT OF IT!
JOSH– PLEASE!

DAD! DAD! OH, I'M SO GLAD TO SEE YOU!

DAD???
IT'S–IT'S JOSH! HE'S BEEN SHOCKED AND HE...
DO SOMETHING, DAD! JOSH IS HURT! WHY AREN'T YOU HELPING ME????
YOU'RE NOT MY FATHER! WHO ARE YOU??
WHO ARE YOU? AAARRRRRRRRUUUU?? HELP MEEERRRRRRR. DRRRRSMMMMMMMMMM

MR. WRIGHT, WHAT HAPPENED TO YOUR TWO ROBOT KIDS?
PROGRAMMING PROBLEMS.
I HAD TO SHUT THE GIRL OFF. HER MEMORY CHIP MUST BE BAD.
THE ERIN ROBOT WAS SUPPOSED TO THINK OF ME AS HER FATHER, BUT JUST NOW SHE DIDN'T RECOGNIZE ME.
WHAT ABOUT THE JOSH ROBOT?
I THINK THE ELECTRICAL SYSTEM SHORTED.
WHAT A SHAME, BUT IT WAS A GREAT IDEA TO MAKE ROBOT KIDS TO TEST THE PARK.
WE'LL REPROGRAM THESE TWO AND TRY THEM OUT ON THE SHOCKER STUDIO TOUR AGAIN...
...BEFORE WE OPEN THE PARK TO REAL KIDS.

THE END

Still with us, I see. I guess you're made of *sterner stuff* than I thought... But mark my words, I'll have the last laugh.
TICKETS
Our next story, *THE WEREWOLF OF FEVER SWAMP*, will really get under your skin. It might even transform you from a brave soul into a gibbering, frightened lunatic!!!
ENJOY!

IT ALL BEGAN WHEN WE MOVED TO **FLORIDA**.
I CAN STILL HEAR MY DAD TELLING US THIS WAS THE CHANCE OF A LIFETIME, AN **ADVENTURE** WE'D NEVER FORGET.
HE COULDN'T HAVE KNOWN BACK THEN HOW RIGHT HE WAS!

HEY, EMILY! LOOK AT THAT!
OUR NEW HOUSE WAS AT THE EDGE OF THE SWAMP. I COULDN'T WAIT TO EXPLORE. I STOOD IN THE BACKYARD WITH THE BINOCULARS MY DAD HAD GIVEN ME FOR MY BIRTHDAY AND GAZED TOWARD THE SWAMP.
IT'S A CRANE.
LET'S FOLLOW IT.

NO WAY. IT'S TOO HOT.
MEET MY SISTER EMILY. SHE CRIED FOR DAYS WHEN WE MOVED HERE FROM VERMONT. SHE DIDN'T WANT TO MISS HER SENIOR YEAR IN HIGH SCHOOL.
EMILY, TAKE A SHORT WALK WITH GRADY. YOU'RE NOT DOING ANYTHING ELSE.
BUT, MOM-
GO AHEAD, EM.
DAD AND MOM ARE BOTH SCIENTISTS. THEY WORK TOGETHER ON A LOT OF PROJECTS.
THEY GOT SIX SWAMP DEER FROM SOUTH AMERICA. THEY WANT TO SEE IF THESE DEER CAN SURVIVE IN THE SWAMPS IN FLORIDA. SO HERE WE ARE, LIVING IN FLORIDA WITH SIX WEIRD-LOOKING DEER IN OUR BACKYARD.
COME ON, EMILY. JUST A SHORT WALK. VERY SHORT.
NO.
IT WILL BE INTERESTING, MORE INTERESTING THAN STANDING AROUND IN THE HEAT ARGUING WITH YOUR BROTHER
WELL ...
GREAT! LET'S GO!

YUCK. GNATS. I HATE GNATS. IT MAKES ME ITCHY JUST TO LOOK AT THEM.
HEY- WHAT WAS THAT?
AN ALLIGATOR! A HUNGRY ALLIGATOR!
WHAT'S YOUR PROBLEM, EM? IT WAS JUST SOME KIND OF LIZARD.
YOU'RE A CREEP, GRADY.
HA, HA, HA!
IT'S TOO ITCHY IN THIS SWAMP. LET'S HEAD BACK.
JUST A LITTLE BIT FARTHER.
HEY- ANOTHER POND!

IT'S QUICKSAND!
WHOAAAA!!!
GOTCHA!
NOT FUNNY!
IT ISN'T QUICKSAND, DORK. IT'S A PEAT BOG.
WHAT'S A PEAT BOG?
THE POND IS THICK BECAUSE IT HAS PEAT MOSS GROWING IN IT. THE MOSS ABSORBS 25 TIMES ITS OWN WEIGHT IN WATER.
IT'S GROSS-LOOKING.
DRINK SOME, SEE HOW IT TASTES.
I'M NOT THIRSTY.
BLORP
LET'S GET GOING. I'M REALLY HOT.

THIS WAY.
ARE YOU SURE? I DON'T THINK WE'VE BEEN HERE BEFORE.
WE BOTH REALIZED WE WERE LOST. COMPLETELY **LOST.**
HEY, LOOK...
DO YOU THINK SOMEONE LIVES HERE? IN THE MIDDLE OF THE SWAMP?
MAYBE HE CAN TELL US WHICH WAY TO GET HOME.
MAYBE.
A...ANYONE HOME?

IT'S A HIDEOUT. A CRIMINAL. A BANK ROBBER. OR A KILLER.
HE'S HIDING HERE.
SHHH!!!!
ANYONE HOME?
ANYONE HOME?
ANYONE IN THERE?
CCCRREEEEAAAKKKK

AAAAA
AAAAA

EMILY! WAIT UP! HE'S CHASING US!
RUN, GRADY, **RUN!**

HEY, THIS LOOKS FAMILIAR. LET'S GO!

HE-HE'S GONE! WE LOST HIM!
WELCOME BACK, EXPLORERS
HOME, SWEET HOME!
WE THOUGHT YOU GOT LOST.
WE DID!
YOU WHAT?
WE GOT LOST AND THEN A MAN CHASED US!
A STRANGE MAN WITH LONG, WHITE HAIR. HE LIVES IN A HUT IN THE MIDDLE OF THE SWAMP!
THE SWAMP HERMIT.
WHO?
THE GUY IN THE HARDWARE STORE TOLD ME ABOUT HIM. HE SAID HE WAS STRANGE, BUT PERFECTLY HARMLESS. BEEN LIVING IN THE SWAMP BY HIMSELF MOST OF HIS LIFE. NO ONE EVEN KNOWS HIS NAME.
MAYBE THEY SHOULDN'T GO BACK IN THE SWAMP BY THEMSELVES.
WELL, I TOLD YOU THIS WAS GOING TO BE AN ADVENTURE.
DON'T WORRY. YOU WON'T CATCH ME BACK IN THAT SWAMP.
COME WITH ME, GRADY. TIME TO FEED THE DEER.

THAT NIGT AFTER DINNER, I FELT A LITTLE HOMESICK.
I THOUGHT ABOUT MY FRIENDS BACK IN VERMONT AND HOW WE USED TO HANG OUT.
I DECIDED TO TAKE A WALK.
HEY!
THE SWAMP HERMIT!!!
I SAW YOU FROM MY YARD. I LIVE OVER THERE. YOU JUST MOVED IN?
YEAH. I'M GRADY TUCKER. WHAT'S YOUR NAME?
WILL. **WILL BLAKE**.
WILL SAID HE WAS MY AGE, BUT HE LOOKED LIKE A FOOTBALL LINEMAN.
HOW LONG HAVE YOU LIVED HERE?
A FEW MONTHS.
ARE THERE ANY OTHER KIDS OUR AGE AROUND?
YEAH. ONE.
BUT SHE'S A GIRL AND SHE'S KIND OF WEIRD.
HAVE YOU BEEN IN THE SWAMP?
YEAH. THIS AFTERNOON. MY SISTER AND I GOT LOST.
DO YOU KNOW WHY IT'S CALLED **FEVER SWAMP**?

YEAH. MY DAD TOLD ME THE STORY. I THINK IT WAS A HUNDRED YEARS AGO. EVERYONE IN TOWN CAME DOWN WITH A STRANGE FEVER.
LOTS OF PEOPLE DIED FROM IT. AND THOSE WHO DIDN'T, BEGAN ACTING VERY STRANGE: TALKING CRAZY, FALLING DOWN OR WALKING AROUND IN CIRCLES.
WEIRD.
EVER SINCE THAT TIME, THEY CALLED IT FEVER SWAMP.
I'VE GOT TO GO. HEY! MAYBE YOU AND I CAN GO EXPLORING IN THE SWAMP TOGETHER.
GREAT!
A FEW NIGHTS LATER, I HEARD THE HOWLS FOR THE FIRST TIME.
AAAAOOOOUL
AAAAOOOOUL
RIGHT OUTSIDE THE WINDOW. LONG, ANGRY HOWLS.

GRADY!
GRADY, IT'S ME, EMILY.
DID YOU HEAR THE HOWLS?
YES, THEY WOKE ME UP. LET'S TAKE A LOOK.
WHAT'S THAT?
SCRATCH SCRATCH
SCRATCH SCRATCH SCRATCH
DO YOU THINK ONE OF THE DEER ESCAPED?
DO YOU REALLY THINK A DEER WOULD SCRATCH AT THE DOOR?
WHAT'S GOING ON HERE?

IT'S PAST MIDNIGHT.
WE HEARD NOISES. HOWLS OUTSIDE.
AND THEN SOMETHING WAS SCRATCHING AT THE DOOR.
MAYBE IT WAS THE WIND.
LET'S CHECK THE DEER.
CLICK
YOU SEE? **NOTHING.**
IT'S HARD TO SLEEP IN A NEW HOUSE. THE SOUNDS ARE ALL SO NEW. BUT YOU'LL GET USED TO THEM.
NO MORE WANDERING AROUND TONIGHT, OKAY?
THE NEXT MORNING WAS SO BEAUTIFUL, I WONDERED IF THE HOWLS WERE JUST PART OF A DREAM.
AKES
WHERE ARE YOU GOING SO EARLY?
I WANT TO SEE IF WILL IS HOME, MOM. MAYBE WE'LL HANG OUT OR SOMETHING.

WHOoAAAAA!!
HELP! HELP! IT'S GOT ME! IT'S...
...LICKING MY FACE?
WHERE'D **YOU** COME FROM?
HE'S ENORMOUS. HE MUST WEIGH MORE THAN A HUNDRED POUNDS.
HE LIKES YOU.
BUT HE PRACTICALLY KILLED ME. HE SCARED ME TO DEATH, DIDN'T YOU, FELLA?
I WONDER WHO HE BELONGS TO. GRADY, CHECK HIS COLLAR.
NOTHING THERE.
MAYBE HE'S A STRAY. MAYBE THAT'S WHY HE WAS SCRATCHING AT THE DOOR LAST NIGHT.

HI!
HI, WILL. LOOK WHAT WE FOUND.
HAVE YOU SEEN THIS DOG BEFORE? DOES HE BELONG TO SOMEONE IN THE NEIGHBORHOOD?
NOPE. NEVER SEEN HIM.
HE LOOKS MORE LIKE A WOLF THAN A DOG.
YEAH. HE REALLY DOES.
LET'S CALL HIM WOLF. SEE? HE LIKES THE NAME! CAN I KEEP HIM?
WE'LL SEE.
THAT NIGHT MY PARENTS AGREED TO LET WOLF SLEEP IN MY ROOM.
I DON'T KNOW HOW LONG I SLEPT BEFORE I WAS AWAKENED BY A SUDDEN
CRASH

CRASH
CLING
BUMP
WOLF! STOP!
BUMP
HE'S TRYING TO GET OUTSIDE!
OPEN THE FRONT DOOR! LET HIM OUT BEFORE HE WRECKS THE HOUSE!
WHAT A MESS HE'S MADE!
HE'S HEADING TO THE SWAMP.
WOLF WILL HAVE TO STAY OUTSIDE.
BUT, DAD...
HE'S TOO BIG AND RESTLESS TO STAY IN THE HOUSE.
NOW MAYBE WE CAN ALL SLEEP IN PEACE.
WRONG.

BECAUSE A SHORT WHILE LATER...
AAAAAOOOUUUUUU
GRRRRRR
GROOAAR
GRRRRAAAR
WOLF???

AAAAAOOOUUUUUU
AFTER BREAKFAST THE NEXT MORNING, I LED DAD OUT TO THE BACKYARD. WHEN I SAW WHAT WAS LYING IN A HEAP ON THE GRASS, I STARTED TO GAG.
IT WAS A **RABBIT** THAT HAD BEEN RIPPED OPEN, NEARLY TORN IN HALF.
I'M GLAD THE DEER ARE SAFE INSIDE THAT PEN.
WOLF!
WOOF! WOOF! WOOF!
WOLF, DOWN! HA, HA HA!
YOUR DOG IS A **KILLER**.

WHAT?
LOOK WHAT HE DID TO THAT POOR BUNNY RABBIT.
WHOA! HOLD ON. WHO SAID WOLF DID **THIS**?
WHO ELSE COULD HAVE DONE IT? HE'S A KILLER.
NO WAY! YOU HAVE NO PROOF!
GRADY, WOLF MAY BE A BIT OF A HUNTER.
BUT, DAD. DIDN'T YOU HEAR THOSE **HOWLS** LAST NIGHT? DOGS DON'T HOWL LIKE THAT.
THEN WHAT WAS IT?
YES, I HEARD THEM. THEY SOUNDED MORE LIKE WOLF HOWLS, OR MAYBE A COYOTE. BUT I'D BE VERY SURPRISED TO FIND THEM IN THIS SWAMP AREA.
LET'S JUST BE CAREFUL AROUND WOLF. HE SEEMS GENTLE, BUT WE REALLY DON'T KNOW ANYTHING ABOUT HIM.
I'M GOING TO STAY AS FAR AWAY FROM THAT **MONSTER** AS I CAN.
DAD GOT A SHOVEL AND BOX TO CARRY AWAY THE DEAD RABBIT IN.

YOU AREN'T A MONSTER, ARE YOU, BOY?
THAT WASN'T YOU I SAW LAST NIGHT, WAS IT?
WOLF SEEMED TO BE TRYING TO TELL ME SOMETHING. BUT I HAD NO IDEA WHAT IT COULD BE.
THAT NIGHT I DIDN'T HEAR THE HOWLS.
I WOKE UP IN THE MIDDLE OF THE NIGHT AND STARED OUT THE WINDOW. WOLF WAS GONE, PROBABLY EXPLORING THE SWAMP.
IN THE MORNING, I KNEW HE'D COME RUNNING BACK TO GREET ME.
HEY, WHAT'S UP?
HI, WILL.
WANT TO GO EXPLORING? YOU KNOW. IN THE SWAMP?
YEAH. SURE.
MOM, I'M GOING TO THE SWAMP WITH WILL.
BE CAREFUL, GRADY.

DID YOU HEAR ABOUT MR. WARNER? HE LIVES WITH HIS WIFE IN THE VERY LAST HOUSE ON THE BLOCK.
WHAT ABOUT HIM?
HE'S MISSING. HE DIDN'T COME HOME LAST NIGHT.
FROM WHERE?
FROM THE SWAMP. MRS. WARNER SAID HE WENT HUNTING WILD TURKEYS IN THE SWAMP YESTERDAY AFTERNOON... AND HE HASN'T COME BACK.
MAYBE HE GOT LOST.
NO WAY. NOT MR. WARNER. HE'S LIVED HERE A LONG TIME. HE WOULDN'T GET LOST.
THEN MAYBE THE WEREWOLF GOT HIM!
CASSIE O'ROURKE! WHAT ARE YOU DOING HERE?
FOLLOWING YOU.

YOU ARE THE NEW KID. GRADY, RIGHT?
HI.
WHAT DID YOU SAY ABOUT A WEREWOLF?
DON'T START WITH THAT STUFF AGAIN. IT'S STUPID.
THERE'S A WEREWOLF IN THE SWAMP!
AND I'M GOING TO FLAP MY WINGS AND FLY TO MARS.
YOU'RE JUST AFRAID, WILL BLAKE!
YOU'VE GOT A GOOD IMAGINATION, CASSIE. I GUESS YOU WATCH A LOT OF SCARY MOVIES.
DO YOU HEAR THE HOWLING SOUNDS AT NIGHT?
YEAH.
THOSE HOWLS **AREN'T HUMAN!** THEY COME FROM A WEREWOLF THAT HAS JUST KILLED!
OOOH! STOP! YOU'RE MAKING ME SHAKE ALL OVER.
THERE'S NO SUCH THING AS **WEREWOLVES**...UNLESS MAYBE YOU'RE ONE!
VERY FUNNY.
WHAT DOES THE WEREWOLF LOOK LIKE? DOES IT HAVE RED HAIR AND FRECKLES?
TH-THERE'S THE WEREWOLF!!

THE SWAMP HERMIT!
IT'S HIM! IT'S THE WEREWOLF!
CASSIE, SHUT UP! HE'LL HEAR YOU!
HE SEES US!
RUN! COME ON! RUN!!!

I'M THE WEREWOLF!!
AAAAAA AAA AAA AAA
AAAAAAA
HA HA HA!
I'M THE
WEREWOLF!!
THUMP
UNGH!

HELP! WILL! CASSIE!
GO ON. GO. JUST TEASING YOU.
W-WHAT?
GO. I'M NOT GOING TO BITE YOU.
YIP!

THIS DOG YOURS?
YEAH. I...FOUND HIM.
WATCH OUT FOR HIM.
W-WATCH OUT FOR HIM?
WHAT DO YOU MEAN?
WOOF!
WOLF - WHY DIDN'T YOU PROTECT ME?
ARE YOU A BIG COWARD? YOU SOUND REAL TOUGH, BUT YOU'RE ACTUALLY A BIG CHICKEN? IS THAT YOUR PROBLEM?

WHAT HAPPENED? WHAT HAPPENED TO GRADY?
HE WAS BITTEN BY A WEREWOLF!
I'M OKAY. I THINK I WAS MAINLY SCARED. LET'S GO HOME.
CASSIE HAS WEREWOLVES ON THE BRAIN. SHE THINKS THE SWAMP HERMIT IS A WEREWOLF.
THAT OLD SWAMP HERMIT IS SUPPOSED TO BE HARMLESS.
WELL, HE GAVE US A REAL SCARE. HE CHASED US THROUGH THE SWAMP, YELLING "I'M THE WEREWOLF!"
YOU SHOULD STAY AWAY FROM HIM.
DO YOU BELIEVE IN WEREWOLVES?
YOUR MOM AND I ARE SCIENTISTS. WE'RE NOT SUPPOSED TO BELIEVE IN SUPERNATURAL THINGS LIKE WEREWOLVES.
YOUR FATHER IS A WEREWOLF. I HAVE TO SHAVE HIS BACK EVERY MORNING SO HE'LL LOOK HUMAN.
I'M SERIOUS. HAVEN'T YOU HEARD THE WEIRD SOUNDS AT NIGHT?
THE HOWLS DIDN'T START UNTIL THAT DOG SHOWED UP. YOUR DOG IS A WEREWOLF!
GIVE ME A BREAK!
ENOUGH WEREWOLF TALK!

THE MOON WILL LOOK FULL FOR ONLY TWO MORE NIGHTS.
IF THE HOWLS STOP AFTER TOMORROW NIGHT, WE'LL KNOW IT WAS A WEREWOLF, HOWLING AT THE FULL MOON.
AAAOOOUUU
AAAAOOUUU
AAAOOUUU

I'M AFRAID YOUR DOG IS A KILLER.

THE NEXT MORNING...
I'M GOING TO HAVE TO TAKE WOLF TO THE POUND.
BUT THEY'LL KILL HIM!
I KNOW HOW YOU FEEL, GRADY. BUT THE DOG IS A KILLER.
IT WASN'T WOLF! I HEARD THE HOWLS!
IT WAS A WEREWOLF, DAD! THERE'S A WEREWOLF IN THE SWAMP! CASSIE WAS RIGHT!
GRADY...
I KNOW I'M RIGHT, DAD! IT'S BEEN A FULL MOON. IT'S A WEREWOLF. THE SWAMP HERMIT! HE DID IT, DAD!!
GRADY, STOP NOW!
GO LOOK AT THE PAW PRINTS ON THE GROUND. I CAN'T TAKE ANY MORE CHANCES.
I HAVE NO CHOICE...

NO!
GRADY!!!
WHA...?!
RUN, WOLF, RUN!
HEY!
GO, BOY GO!

THAT WAS DUMB, GRADY.
WOLF WILL COME BACK LATER. WHEN HE DOES, I'LL HAVE TO TAKE HIM AWAY.
BUT, DAD-
NO MORE DISCUSSION.
COME HELP ME GET THE DEER PEN PATCHED UP.
ALL DAY LONG, I WATCHED THE SWAMP. I FELT NERVOUS, SHAKY.
BY EVENING, WOLF HADN'T RETURNED.
MY WHOLE FAMILY WAS TENSE. AT DINNER, WE HARDLY SPOKE.
I WENT TO BED EARLY. I WAS REALLY TIRED FROM BEING UP MOST OF THE NIGHT BEFORE.
IT WAS THE LAST NIGHT OF THE FULL MOON, BUT HEAVY BLANKETS OF CLOUDS COVERED THE MOONLIGHT.
I SETTLED MY HEAD INTO THE PILLOW AND TRIED TO SLEEP.
THEN THE HOWLS STARTED...

AAOOOUL
WOLF!
GRRRRRR
HE WAS PACING AND GROWLING, AS IF SOMETHING WAS REALLY TROUBLING HIM...
OR SCARING HIM!
I FUMBLED INTO MY SNEAKERS. I HAD TO FOLLOW WOLF.
I'M GOING TO PROVE ONCE AND FOR ALL HE ISN'T A KILLER OR A WEREWOLF.

CRACK
HEY! WHO'S THERE?
GRADY- IT'S YOU!
WILL- WHAT ARE YOU DOING OUT HERE?
I HEARD THE HOWLS. I DECIDED TO INVESTIGATE.
ME, TOO. I'M GLAD TO SEE YOU! WE CAN EXPLORE TOGETHER.
LOOK! THERE'S WOLF!

HE WENT THIS WAY! FOLLOW ME!
HEY, WILL?
WILL???

CRACKLE
WILL, IS THAT YOU? WHERE ARE YOU?
THE SWAMP HERMIT? OH, NO!
NO! NO!
NO!

GRRAOOOORR
UNGH!
THUMP

YOU SHOULDN'T HAVE COME TO THE SWAMP AT NIGHT, GRADY ...
NOT WHEN THE MOON IS FULL!!
W...WILL?
AAAOOUUUU
WILL! NO! WILL-!
AAAAAAAA
CHOMP

WOLF!
WOOF WOOF WOOF GRRRR
GRAAAH
WOLF! I KNEW IT WASN'T YOU. IT WAS WILL...
...ALL ALONG!

THAT WAS A MONTH AGO.
THE LAST THING I REMEMBER THEN IS SEEING **WILL** RUN AWAY ON ALL FOURS. **WOLF** FOLLOWED. I HEARD WILL UTTER A CRY OF PAIN, A WAIL OF DEFEAT.
I SANK DOWN INTO BLUE-BLACK DARKNESS . . .
. . . AND WOKE UP IN MY OWN BEDROOM.
HOW- HOW DID I GET HERE?

WILL WAS GONE.
BUT I KNOW I'LL NEVER FORGET HIM. HE CHANGED MY LIFE.
I'M STANDING AT MY BEDROOM WINDOW NOW, WATCHING THE FULL MOON RISING THROUGH THE TREES.
CASSIE WAS RIGHT. WHEN A WEREWOLF BITES YOU, HE PASSES ON THE CURSE.
AAAOOOUUUU

THE END

Well, well, well.
You survived after all.
No matter.
There's more where that came from! ***HA-HA!***
Here lies Dear Reader RIP

Here lies
Dear
Reader
RIP

Next we have a tale of *ghastly woe* to make even the toughest person quake with fear. The title is *GHOST BEACH,* and it's a scream!

So read on, if you *dare*. Just don't come crying to me when it gets to be too much!

I DON'T REMEMBER HOW WE GOT TO THE GRAVEYARD.
IN MEMORY OF
JOHN,
SON OF DANIEL
SARAH KNAPP,
WHO DIED
THE SKY GREW DARK AND THEN WE WERE THERE.
WEIRD, I THOUGHT.
THIS KID WAS MY AGE WHEN HE DIED.
IN MEMORY OF
JOHN
SON OF DANIEL
AND SARAH KNAPP
WHO DIED
MARCH 25TH, 1766
AGE 12 YEARS

TERRI? WHERE DID YOU GO?
YOU'RE GOING THE WRONG WAY. I'M OVER HERE.
IT'S GETTING DARK. LET'S GET OUT OF...
...HERE.
I LET OUT A SCREAM.

BUT I WAS ALREADY RUNNING.
JERRY! THEY'VE GOT ME!
IT WON'T LET GO!
WE WERE BOTH TRAPPED.

GROSS.
MAYBE YOU REMEMBERED THAT DREAM BECAUSE YOU'RE NERVOUS ABOUT BEING AWAY FROM HOME.
MAYBE. BUT WHAT COULD HAPPEN? AGATHA AND BRAD ARE GREAT.
BRAD SADLER IS OUR DISTANT COUSIN, ANCIENT DISTANT COUSIN IS MORE LIKE IT. AGATHA IS HIS WIFE.
DAD SAID THEY WERE OLD WHEN HE WAS A KID.
BUT THEY'RE BOTH FUN AND ENERGETIC DESPITE THEIR AGE.

SO WHEN THEY INVITED US TO SPEND THE SUMMER IN THEIR COTTAGE NEAR THE BEACH, TERRI AND I EAGERLY SAID YES.
WHY DON'T YOU KIDS HAVE A LOOK AROUND? THERE'S A LOT TO EXPLORE.
SO HERE WE ARE, CHECKING THINGS OUT.
JERRY- LOOK! UP THERE!
LET'S GO-
WHOOOOO- WHAT WAS THAT?
LET'S CLIMB UP AND EXPLORE.
I WONDER IF SOMEONE LIVES IN IT.
WHOOOOOO!
SOMETIMES TERRI CAN BE SUCH A DORK.

WHOA!
SHOOOOMMM
HEY! WHERE'D IT GO?
CRUNCH
STAY AWAY. IF YOU GET RABIES, YOU'LL GET ME IN TROUBLE.
THANKS FOR YOUR CONCERN.
WHAT THE--?

LOOK OUT! IT BITES!
WHA-!?!
YOU CAN COME OUT NOW.
Hee-hee!
Heh-heh!
VERY FUNNY.
WHO ARE YOU?
WE'RE ALL SADLERS. I'M SAM.
THAT'S LOUISA. THAT'S NAT.
DO YOU KNOW OUR COUSINS? BRAD AND AGATHA?
SURE. THIS IS A SMALL PLACE. EVERYONE KNOWS EVERYONE ELSE.
WOW. WE'RE SADLERS, TOO.

WHAT DO YOU DO FOR FUN AROUND HERE?
PLAY GAMES. PICK BLUEBERRIES. COME DOWN TO THE WATER.
DO YOU EVER GO EXPLORING UP THERE?
WE NEVER GO NEAR THERE.
ARE YOU KIDDING?
WHY NOT?
DO YOU BELIEVE IN GHOSTS?

NO WAY! COME ON!
YOU MEAN THERE ARE GHOSTS IN THERE?
WE'VE GOT TO GO NOW.
HEY, WAIT. WE WANT TO HEAR ABOUT THE GHOSTS!
THERE ARE SO MANY GHOST STORIES FROM AROUND THE WORLD, HOW CAN GHOSTS NOT BE REAL?

MAYBE THAT'S WHY I GET SCARED IN STRANGE PLACES.
OF COURSE, I'D NEVER ADMIT IT TO TERRI. SHE'D LAUGH AT ME FOREVER.
TERRI! COME HERE!
IS IT H-HUMAN?
NOT UNLESS THE HUMAN HAD FOUR LEGS. MY GUESS IS IT'S A DOG.
OH, POOR LITTLE DOGGY. HOW DO YOU THINK IT DIED?
OLD AGE?
OR MAYBE ANOTHER ANIMAL ATTACKED IT?
ARRR
ROOOOOOOOOOOOO!
WHAT'S THAT?
A SHRILL ANIMAL HOWL FILLED THE FOREST.
I DIDN'T KNOW.

YOU TWO ARE EASY TO SCARE.
THESE JOKES ARE GETTING PRETTY LAME.
LOOK!
A GHOST KILLED THIS DOG!
SHUSH, IT'S ALL RIGHT.
DOGS CAN TELL IF SOMEONE'S A GHOST. THEY ALWAYS BARK WARNINGS.
THERE'S NO SUCH THING AS-
YOU'RE WRONG.

THESE WOODS ARE FULL OF SKELETONS, ALL BECAUSE OF THE GHOST. HE PICKS THEM CLEAN.
TELL US MORE. OR IS THIS ANOTHER ONE OF YOUR FABULOUS JOKES?
MAYBE SOME OTHER TIME.
WAIT! I WANT TO HEAR MORE.
IS THIS THE GHOST IN THE CAVE? HAVE YOU SEEN IT?
YOU CAN SEE FLICKERING LIGHTS SOMETIMES.
WELL, A FLICKERING LIGHT AND A DOG SKELETON AREN'T ENOUGH TO CONVINCE ME. NICE TRY.

WHAT'D YOU DO THAT FOR? I WAS JUST WEASELING SOME GOOD STUFF OUT OF THEM.
SOCK
CAN'T YOU SEE? IT'S JUST ANOTHER DUMB JOKE.
THERE'S NO GHOST.
DESPITE THE HEAT, A CHILL RAN DOWN MY BACK.
WAS THERE A GHOST?
DID I REALLY WANT TO FIND OUT?

OVER DINNER, WE TOLD AGATHA AND BRAD ABOUT SAM, NAT, AND LOUISA.
THEY SAID THEY KNOW YOU.
YEP. NEIGHBORS.

THEY SAID A GHOST MUST HAVE KILLED THAT DOG.
THOSE KIDS WERE TEASING YOU. THEY LOVE GHOST STORIES.
ESPECIALLY THAT SAM.
HOPE YOU LIKE PEACH PIE.
SAM SAYS THE GHOST LIVES IN THE CAVE.
DID HE?
YOU DIDN'T GO IN THERE, DID YOU?
IT ISN'T SAFE.
SAM SAYS HE'S SEEN FLICKERING LIGHTS IN THE CAVE.
IT HAPPENS A FEW TIMES A YEAR. SOMETHING ELECTRIC IN THE AIR.

I SEEM TO BE MISSING A BEACH TOWEL.
DID WE LEAVE ONE ON THE BEACH?
I CAN GO LOOK.
IT'S GETTING DARK. YOU CAN LOOK TOMORROW.
I DON'T MIND.
I WAS GLAD FOR AN EXCUSE TO ESCAPE AND BE ALONE FOR A CHANGE.
TERRI IS OKAY FOR A KID SISTER. BUT SOMETIMES I LIKE TO BE BY MYSELF.

HUH? IS THAT A LIGHT?
IT HAD TO BE THE REFLECTION OF THE MOON.
NO, NOT THE MOON. SAM.
YES, IT'S SAM. HE'S UP THERE RIGHT NOW, LIGHTING MATCHES.

WHA!?!

WHAT DO YOU THINK YOU'RE DOING!
DO YOU SEE THAT LIGHT?

WHAT LIGHT?

LET'S GO IN.
MY HEART THUDDED AS WE STEPPED INTO THE DARKNESS.
CHITTER
CHITTER
WHAT'S THAT NOISE?
AGHHH!
NOOOOO-!
THIS IS WHY BRAD AND AGATHA WARNED US AWAY.
LET'S GET OUT OF HERE. I HATE BATS!
THE LIGHT-LOOK!

JUST A FEW FEET DEEPER... INTO THE CHAMBER.
AND WE COULD SOLVE THE MYSTERY.
SO THAT EXPLAINS IT. CANDLELIGHT.
IT DOESN'T EXPLAIN ANYTHING.
WHO PUT ALL THESE CANDLES HERE?
WE BOTH SAW THE OLD MAN AT THE SAME TIME.
SHADOWS PLAYED OVER HIM IN THE FLICKERING CANDLELIGHT.
WAS HE ALIVE?
WAS HE A GHOST?

HIS VOICE WAS A DRY WHISPER... DRY AS DEATH!
COME HERE.
GO! GO! GO!!!
MY LEGS FELT AS IF THEY WEIGHED A THOUSAND POUNDS.
THE BLOOD PULSED SO HARD AT MY TEMPLES, I THOUGHT MY HEAD MIGHT EXPLODE.
HE WAS COMING AFTER US!
I COULD HEAR HIM GROAN AS HE REACHED OUT HIS BONY HAND.
THEN WE WERE SLIPPING, SLIDING, SCRAMBLING DOWN TO THE ROCKY BEACH...AND HOME.

TERRI? JERRY? IS THAT YOU?
DID YOU FIND IT?
HUH?
THE BEACH TOWEL-DID YOU FIND IT?
TAP TAP TAP
WE COULDN'T GET TO SLEEP THAT NIGHT. I KEPT PICTURING THE GHOST'S SUNKEN EYES AND WONDERING IF WE SHOULD TELL AGATHA AND BRAD WHAT HAPPENED.
THEY PROBABLY WON'T BELIEVE US ANYWAY.
AND WE'D JUST GET IN TROUBLE FOR GOING INTO THE CAVE.
COME HERE...
HAD THE GHOST FOLLOWED US HOME?
NAT? YOU SCARED US TO DEATH!
WOW!
...SO WE SAW THE GHOST. HE WAS VERY OLD AND SCARY-LOOKING. HE KIND OF FLOATED UP AND THEN STARTED CHASING US.

WE DIDN'T WANT YOU TO KNOW ABOUT THE GHOST. WE DIDN'T WANT TO SCARE YOU.
YOU'VE SEEN HIM, TOO?
WE STAY AWAY FROM THERE. THE GHOST IS TOO SCARY.
HE'S REALLY DANGEROUS. HE WANTS TO KILL US ALL.
EVEN YOU. NOBODY'S SAFE. YOU SAW THAT SKELETON IN THE WOODS.
THAT'S WHAT HE'LL DO IF HE CATCHES YOU.
THERE IS A WAY TO GET RID OF THE GHOST. BUT WE NEED YOUR HELP.
THE NEXT MORNING WE HURRIED TO THE BEACH. THERE WAS NO SIGN OF SAM, NAT AND LOUISA. SO WE WALKED HOME, CUTTING THROUGH A LITTLE CEMETERY.

HERE LIES THE BODY OF MARTIN SADLER
THAT'S *STRANGE.*
MARY SADLER BELOVED WIFE OF MARTIN
PETER SADLER BELOVED SON
MIRIAM SADLER BELOVED DAUGHTER
ALL SADLERS, *TOO.*
HIRAM, MARGARET, CONSTANCE, CHARITY...
I WAS STARTING TO GET THE *CREEPS.*
JERRY! OVER *HERE!*
YEAH, I *KNOW.* THE WHOLE *CEMETERY* IS FILLED WITH...
SADLERS...
SAM SADLER 1629 - 1641
LOUISA SADLER
NATHANIAL SADLER
REST IN PEACE

THREE STONES. THREE KIDS.
THOSE ARE OUR ANCESTORS.
WE WERE *NAMED* AFTER THEM.
LOTS OF SADLERS AROUND HERE WERE NAMED FOR ANCESTORS, EVEN YOUR *COUSINS*.
SEE?
AGATHA SADLER
BRADFORD SADLER
OKAY, *FINE*. NOW, YOU SAID YOU HAD A PLAN TO GET RID OF THE GHOST.
WE DO. COME WITH *US*.
SEE ALL THOSE BIG ROCKS PILED ON TOP OF THE CAVE?

HE'S A GHOST! HE COULD JUST FLOAT THROUGH THE ROCKS!
ALL YOU HAVE TO DO IS PUSH THEM DOWN. THE OLD GHOST WILL BE TRAPPED INSIDE FOREVER.
THE OLD LEGENDS SAY THE CAVE IS A SANCTUARY. IF SOMETHING EVIL GETS TRAPPED INSIDE, IT CAN'T ESCAPE THROUGH THE ANCIENT ROCKS.
SO WHY DON'T YOU DO IT?
WE'RE TOO SCARED.
WE LIVE HERE. IF WE MESS UP, THE GHOST COULD FIND OUR HOUSE AND GET REVENGE.
WILL YOU HELP US?
PLEASE? HE'S TERRIFIED US OUR WHOLE LIVES!
OF COURSE WE'LL HELP YOU.

WERE WE REALLY GOING TO TRAP A GHOST TONIGHT?
WHAT IF THE ROCKS WON'T BUDGE? WHAT IF WE SLIP AND FALL?
WHAT IF THE GHOST DOES FLOAT OUT?

WE'RE IN DEEP TROUBLE NOW. ALL FIVE OF US!
READY?
WE'LL WAIT DOWN HERE.
MY LEGS FELT RUBBERY AS WE CLIMBED THE DAMP ROCKS.
IF THE GHOST COMES OUT, WE'LL DISTRACT HIM.
ONE SLIP WOULD CAUSE A ROCK SLIDE... AND THE GHOST WOULD KNOW SOMETHING WAS UP.
WHAT'S WRONG? WHY ARE THEY WAVING?

THEY'RE TRYING TO TELL US SOMETHING.
SOMETHING'S GONE WRONG!
LET'S GET OUT OF-
...HERE...

COME WITH ME.
THE GHOST WAS STRONG FOR SOMEONE SO OLD AND FRAIL LOOKING.
WH-WHAT ARE YOU GOING TO DO WITH US?
W-WE DIDN'T MEAN ANY HARM.
IT'S DANGEROUS TO GET INVOLVED WITH GHOSTS.
WE'LL GO AWAY. WE'LL NEVER COME BACK.
WE WON'T TELL ANYONE WE SAW YOU.
ME?
I'M NOT A GHOST.

YOUR THREE *FRIENDS* ARE!
YOU'RE TRYING TO TRICK US. THOSE KIDS–
THEY'RE NOT KIDS.
THEY'RE OVER 350 YEARS OLD.

ALLOW ME TO INTRODUCE MYSELF.
I'M *HARRISON* SADLER.
ANOTHER *SADLER!*
WE'RE SADLERS, TOO.

I KNOW. I CAME HERE AFTER COLLEGE TO TRACE MY ANCESTORS AND TO STUDY... *GHOSTS!*

TURNS OUT THERE'S PLENTY TO STUDY HERE.
WHY DID YOU DRAG US HERE?
TO WARN YOU ABOUT THE GHOSTS.

I'VE BEEN *WATCHING* THEM.
I'VE SEEN THEIR *EVIL.*

THIS PLACE IS A SANCTUARY. ONCE TRAPPED INSIDE, GHOSTS CANNOT ESCAPE THROUGH THE STONE.
SANCTUARY? WASN'T THAT THE WORD SAM USED?
I PLAN TO TRAP THE GHOSTS HERE. THAT'S WHY I STACKED THOSE ROCKS ABOVE THE ENTRANCE. I'M SAFE WITHIN THESE WALLS. THE GHOSTS CAN'T SURPRISE ME.
DIDN'T YOU WONDER WHY THEY SENT YOU INSTEAD OF COMING IN THEMSELVES?
THEY'RE TERRIFIED OF YOU!
YOU DON'T BELIEVE ME.
WHAT ARE YOU GOING TO DO WITH US?
I'M GOING TO LET YOU GO.
GO TO THE OLD GRAVEYARD...
...TO THE EAST CORNER.
ONCE YOU'VE SEEN IT, YOU'LL COME BACK.

SAM, LOUISA AND NAT WERE OUR *FRIENDS*. THERE WAS NO *WAY* THEY WERE GHOSTS.
NO *WAY!*
HARRISON SADLER WAS A *LIAR,* A 350-YEAR-OLD GHOST OF A LIAR.
HE'S-HE'S SO *SCARY.*
I CAN'T BELIEVE HE LET US GO.
I KNOW WHAT HE WANTS US TO SEE.
LOUISA SADLER 1630 - 1641
NATHANIAL SADLER DIED IN HIS FIFTH YEAR
BUT WE ALREADY KNOW THE TRUTH ABOUT THESE OLD GRAVES.
WHOA! IS THAT FRESH DIRT OVER THERE?
BUT NO ONE'S BEEN BURIED HERE IN 50 YEARS. I CHECKED.
TERRI WAS RIGHT: NO ONE HAD BEEN RECENTLY BURIED... *YET!*
WHAT DO THE *MARKERS* SAY?

JERRY? WHAT DO THEY SAY?
JERRY SADLER
TERRI SADLER
LET'S GET OUT OF HERE. WE HAVE TO TELL AGATHA AND BRAD!
WHERE ARE YOU GOING?
W-WE'RE GOING BACK TO THE COTTAGE–
DID YOU KILL THE GHOST?
NO...HE... WHAT DO YOU MEAN, KILL THE GHOST?
WE RAN AWAY. YOU DIDN'T DO A VERY GOOD JOB DISTRACTING HIM.
WE GOT SCARED.
WE THOUGHT THE GHOST GOT YOU.
YOU HAVE TO KILL THE GHOST! YOU HAVE TO!

ARE YOU TOTALLY CRAZY? HOW COULD YOU AGREE TO THIS?
WE HAVE TO SOLVE THE MYSTERY.
THIS ISN'T ONE OF YOUR MYSTERY BOOKS, THIS IS REAL LIFE!
I NEED TO KNOW THE TRUTH.
THE TRUTH IS, WE MIGHT GET KILLED!
WE'LL WAIT HERE.
YOU CAN'T HELP US FROM DOWN HERE. COME UP TO THE CAVE ENTRANCE.
NO! THE GHOST! HE'LL GET US! HE'LL EAT US UP!
WE CAN'T GO UP THERE UNLESS YOU COME UP AND HELP US.
WE DON'T MEAN TO BE SO FRIGHTENED. IT'S JUST WE'VE BEEN AFRAID OF HIM OUR WHOLE LIVES.

LET'S JUST WARM UP INSIDE FOR A MOMENT.
NO, WE CAN'T.
JUST FOR A SECOND, JUST TO WIPE THE RAIN FROM OUR EYES.
WE'RE TOO SCARED.
NOOOoo!
THIS IS THE DUMBEST THING I'VE EVER DONE. I'LL NEVER FORGIVE TERRI.
NEVER!
YOU BROUGHT THE GHOSTS. THANK YOU.

YOU'RE THE GHOST!
YOU'VE TERRIFIED PEOPLE LONG ENOUGH... MORE THAN 300 YEARS!
IT'S TIME FOR YOU TO REST.
HE'S CRAZY! DON'T LISTEN TO HIM!
DON'T LET HIM FOOL YOU! LOOK AT HIS EYES! HE'S LYING TO YOU!
DON'T HURT US!
WHO WAS THE GHOST? HARRISON? OR OUR THREE FRIENDS?
MY SISTER WAS RISKING OUR LIVES JUST TO SOLVE THE MYSTERY. SHE REALLY WAS CRAZY.
HARRISON PUCKERED HIS DRY LIPS AND WHISTLED. MY HEART SKIPPED A BEAT.

A LOW, DARK FIGURE LOPED TOWARDS US, UTTERING A LOW, MENACING GROWL. A MONSTER?
A DOG!
THEN I REMEMBERED...
DOGS RECOGNIZE GHOSTS!
BARK! BARK!
THEY'RE THE GHOSTS.
BARK!
BARK!

YOU-?
WE NEVER HAD A CHANCE. THAT FIRST WINTER, SO LONG AGO...
WE SAILED HERE WITH OUR PARENTS TO START A NEW LIFE.
BUT WE ALL DIED IN THE COLD!
IT WASN'T FAIR! WE BARELY HAD A LIFE AT ALL!
STAY WITH US, COUSINS!
WE DUG SUCH NICE GRAVES FOR YOU, CLOSE TO OURS.
PLAY WITH ME.
I DON'T WANT YOU TO GO...EVER!

STAY BACK!
WHOOSH
I COULD FEEL BODIES MOVING, HEAR THE WHISPERED PLEAS OF THE GHOSTS.
A COLD HAND GRIPPED ME.
AAAAAHHH!
RUN, JERRY! RUN!
KRAKK
RUN! RUN!
THE GROUND SHOOK. THUNDER DROWNED HER SHOUTS.
NO. NOT THUNDER... ROCKS!
RUMMMMMBLE

WE PEERED UP AT THE CAVE AND WAITED.
NO ONE CAME OUT.
IT WAS OVER.
MYSTERY SOLVED.
WHERE WERE YOU?
BRAD AND I WERE WORRIED SICK!
IT'S KIND OF A LONG STORY ...
START AT THE BEGINNING. THAT'S USUALLY THE BEST PLACE.
TERRI AND I DID OUR BEST TO EXPLAIN THE WHOLE STORY.

AS WE TALKED, I COULD SEE THEIR EXPRESSIONS CHANGING.
WE'RE REALLY SORRY.

THE IMPORTANT THING IS THAT YOU'RE SAFE.

JERRY, LOOK. HARRISON SADLER'S DOG.

BARK!
BARK!
HE MUST HAVE ESCAPED AND FOLLOWED US-

BARK!
WHOA!
EASY, BOY. I'M YOUR FRIEND, REMEMBER?
BARK!

I'M NOT A...
...GHOST...

BAD DOG!
NOW YOU'VE GIVEN AWAY OUR SECRET!
WHAT A PITY.
NOW WHAT DO WE DO WITH THESE TWO KIDS, BRAD?
WHAT DO WE DO WITH THESE KIDS?
THE END

Are you still alive, or has *fear* frozen the blood in your veins? Fortunately for you, I've saved the best for last, and it will *haunt* your *dreams*.
It's a fun but fearsome little story called *NIGHT OF THE LIVING DUMMY*, about a couple of my favorite slaves and how they were lucky enough to get to know *me*, your humble narrator.

So let's dive in shall we? By now I'm sure you are all just *dying* with anticipation!
MWA-HA-HA! HA-HA-HA-HA-HA-HA!!!

My sister Lindy and I may be twins, but we never had much in common, until one fateful day...
TOO SLOW, KRIS! YOU'LL NEVER CATCH ME!
WILL TOO!
No one's around! Let's check out the new house! Last one in is a rotten egg!
You sure no one's working today?
It smells great! All the sawdust! So piney!
Watch out for nails! If you step on one you'll get lockjaw and die!
You wish!
SHH! Did you hear that?
CLOMP CLOMP
Maybe someone IS here?

It was just a dumb squirrel.
You sure?
That was a pretty loud squirrel.
OVER HERE! I FOUND SOMETHING!
RUMMAGE
What is it?
RUMMAGE
A child?
IS IT--IS HE...ALIVE?
No, not alive...

I'M A DUMMY, YOU DUMMY!
Someone threw out a perfectly good ventriloquist dummy. Can you believe it?
Ew! He's probably filled with bugs!
Throw him back, Lindy!
She's keeping me!
My name is Slappy!
Why Slappy?
Come over here...
...and I'll SLAP you!

I can't believe you brought that ugly thing to school!
I'm not ugly, *you're* ugly.
He belongs in the dumpster.
I'll put *you* in the dumpster.
Slappy sure is mean!
You're just jealous because I found him and you didn't.
Fine. Go ahead and make a fool of yourself.
Cool! Where did you get him?
Do his eyes move?
Do *your* eyes move?
HA! He looks so lifelike!
Can't say the same for your friend.
HA HA HA
What a riot!
I'll be here all day.

I just got off the phone with Mrs. Marshall down the block.
Does she want you to baby-sit?
She wants me to perform at Amy's birthday party with Slappy!
She's going to pay me twenty dollars!
Honey! Your first job! Congratulations!
And when word gets around, I'll probably perform at a *LOT* of parties and earn even more money!
I better start putting together an act! I'm gonna be rich!
You mean ***we're*** gonna be rich! I'm the brains; you're just the muscle.
Right! Together, Slappy and I are gonna make serious bank!

You're looking glum this evening.
Can I get a dummy, too?
You really want one?
Want what?
Kris says she wants a dummy, too.
NO WAY! Why do you want to be such a copycat?
Why don't you find something of your OWN for once?!
If you can do it, I can do it!
I really think I'd be better at ventriloquism.
I mean, Lindy isn't very funny.
Everyone thinks I'm funny!
Yeah, we're hilarious!

Well, I just think if Lindy has one, I should have one, too.
Girls, please don't fight over a dummy!
COPYCAT! COPYCAT! COPYCAT!
ENOUGH!!!
Lindy, please let your sister play with Slappy.
But Mom!
After you share him for a while, I'm sure one of you will lose interest in him. Maybe both of you.
I don't mind sharing. Can I hold Slappy for just a second?
Beat it, Kris!
I SAID GET LOST, STUPID!
SLAP

Ow! That hurt, Lindy!
Me? I didn't do it, Slappy did!
Why were you so rude to Kris?
Lindy, stop acting dumb and apologize to your sister.
I'm sorry.
No, in your own voice. Slappy didn't hurt Kris, you did.
Okay, okay. I'm sorry.
Here.
How does his mouth work?
There's a string in his back, inside the slit in his jacket. You just pull it. HMPH

I went to bed that night, thinking I had gotten my way...
GASP!
What a strange dream!
Z
Why does Slappy have to grin like that?

The next day, after coming home from chorus rehearsal.
What the--
Do you like the new dummy?
There's a tiny pawnshop on the corner across from my office. I was walking past, and believe it or not, this guy was in the window.
#1
He was cheap, too!
I think the pawnbroker was glad to be rid of him.
His clothes are way cooler than Slappy's!
So you like him?
I *LOVE* him! ***THANKS, MOM!***

Meet Mr. Wood!
Where'd you get that?
YIP?
From Mom! I'm going to start practicing after dinner, I'm going to be a better ventriloquist than you!
Yeah, well I already have three gigs with Slappy, and you're just getting started.
Does everything have to be a competition with you two? Maybe you two could team up? Do a sister act!
I guess, maybe, if Lindy can keep up!
HMPH
Why can't I have something only for me?

Mr. Wood, why were you standing in front of the mirror with your eyes closed?
Well, I wanted to see what I look like when I'm asleep!
How was that joke?
Better than the last one, I guess?
SIGH I need some good joke books, then I'd be ready to perform. Because I'm a pretty good ventriloquist, right?
Um...
Well, I don't move my lips much, do I?
Not too much.
You're hurting Mr. Wood's feelings.
Why do you want to mess with that thing anyway?
Because it's fun!
And I guess I want to show Lindy that I'm better than she is.
Well, good luck with that!
I think I better be getting home!

Where have you been?
Over at Alice's.
Some kids were over, and I practiced Slappy's new rap routine.
Alice spit chocolate milk out of her nose!
THE JOKE IS ON YOU
That's nice.
SHUFFLE
Guess you and Slappy are ready for Amy's big birthday party on Saturday.
TOTALLY!
Aw, they look so cute together.
Are you getting any better with Mr. Wood?
Yeah, I did some stuff for Cody in the park. Made him laugh so hard he couldn't breathe.
Weird. I never thought Cody had much of a sense of humor. But that's great. I can't wait to see how your act stacks up.

The next morning...
OH, NO!
GASP!
Lindy? What is it?
L--LOOK! Mr. Wood he's...
...torn Slappy apart!

Kris, why would you do this?
Huh? What?!
I know you're jealous of Slappy and me--
Wait a minute! Don't accuse me!
Fine. I'll blame that evil dummy of yours...
What did you say?
Nothing.
Something weird is going on... and it's creeping me out.
?
Because if we didn't move the dummies...
...who did?

By late afternoon, everything seemed like it was back to normal, except Lindy was being unusually "helpful."
Tilt his head forward. If you bounce him up and down a little, it'll make him look like he's laughing.
But don't move his mouth so much!
Just so you know, everyone at school thinks that you are both weirdos.
Who cares. They're all weird, too.
And so are you!
Kris, I can still see your lips move!
Anways, Mrs. Berman doesn't think I'm weird. She asked me and Mr. Wood to be MC's for the spring concert!
High profile!
HMPH

I'd better give Kris some pointers, so she's ready for her big break.
Hey, give him back!
STOP BEING A JERK!
HUH?
STUPID JERK!
STUPID JERK!
Lindy! Stop it!
I... CAN'T!
GET LOST! STUPID MORON!!!
LINDY-- STOP IT!
JERK FACE!!!
Let's get out of here...
SCRAM! LOSER! IDIOT!
HE'S SPEAKING FOR HIMSELF!

He's talking on his own?
JERK!
I-I think so! I'm all mixed up!
HERE! TAKE HIM!
HE'S YOURS. MAYBE YOU CAN CONTROL HIM!
TOSS
BRAT!
OH, NO! THE PARTY! I'm going to be late! And I still need to stop at the house to grab Slappy!
But Lindy!
Sorry! Gotta run! If I were you I'd keep a safe distance from that evil dummy!
Mr. Wood isn't REALLY evil...
IS HE?!

I tried to tell Mom what happened, but she totally misunderstood.
I'm tired of these silly competitions!
If you can't be mature, I'll take the dummies away.
Both of them!
BUT MOM!
END OF TOPIC!
I think I'll put you in the closet. Just for tonight.
Nice and cozy, right?
SLAM
I hope he's not mad at me.

Later...
How'd it go?
Slappy and I were a hit! They couldn't get enough of us!
They liked me, hated Lindy.
I'm glad it went okay.
It was better than okay. Mrs. Evans was there, the woman who works for Channel 3.
Seriously?
Yeah! And she thinks my routine is good enough for ***West Coast's Got Talent!***
That's great. Just great.
Where is my share of the loot?
There will be enough for both of us, Slappy. Don't fret.
So where's that weird dummy of yours?
SHIVER

THUD
Kris?
Where are you going at this hour of the night?
SQUEAK
Throat is dry, so I'm heading down to get a drink of water.
'Kay...
TOSS
ARGGH!

Kris? Are you okay?
Kris?
Who would do this...?
MR. WOOD...?!

BARK! BARK!
I don't believe this!
I just came down for a drink and found this mess! The food! My jewelry! Everything!
Mr. Wood did it! Look at him!
STOP IT! STOP IT! THIS IS JUST SICK!
I'm going to take the dummies away from you both! This whole thing has just gotten out of control!
NO!
LAP LAP
THAT'S NOT FAIR!
But I didn't do anything!
I need Mr. Wood for the spring concert! Everyone is counting on me!

You both swear you didn't do it, right?
YES!
Then one of you is lying, and you both lose your dummies.
What if we put everything back right now? Make the kitchen spotless. Can we keep our dummies?
We'll replace all the spoiled groceries with our allowance! Please give us one more chance!
The kitchen better be spotless by morning! And I don't want to hear any more arguments or competitions. No more blaming everything on dummies. I don't want to hear anything about them. EVER!
YOU WON'T!
NOT ANOTHER WORD!

We worked in silence.
Until the kitchen was finally clean.
Think it will pass inspection?
Let's hope so.
SCRUNCH
This dummy has been nothing but trouble.
I'm beginning to really hate you, Mr. Wood.
STOMP
CREAK
Hate you. And ***fear*** you.

SLAM
YAWN!
Night, Kris.
Night,
Lindy.

KNOCK
KNOCK
KNOCK
Psst...Lindy... Did you hear that?
I guess not.
Probably just the wind.
Or my imagination.
THUMP
LET ME OUT!
THUMP
LET ME OUT!!!
BANG
THUMP

Lindy! Did you hear that? Mr. Wood was calling to me! He was talking!
It's just a dream. Go back to bed.
SHAKE SHAKE
IT'S NOT A DREAM! I'VE BEEN AWAKE THE WHOLE TIME!
You're really scared, aren't you?
SOMETHING H--HORRIBLE IS GOING ON HERE!
Yes, and I know who is behind it all.
WHO?
I AM!

But--why?!
For fun! I wanted to see if I could scare you!
I can't believe you fell for that voice in the closet just now! I must be a really good ventriloquist!
But Lindy!
You should have seen your face when you found Mr. Wood downstairs!
How did you ever think of such a mean joke?
It just came to me when you had to go and be a copy-cat with your own dummy.
I can't believe I was so stupid.
Neither can I.
It was too mean to be just a joke. I'm never speaking to you again!
Fine. Just proves what I've always said...
You have no sense of humor.

I didn't have time to plot my revenge on Lindy, because before I knew it, the spring concert had arrived!
EEP!
Kris, you go on in two minutes!
At least Mr. Wood doesn't look nervous.
You ready, old pal?
What's this?
CRINKLE
Has this been in your pocket the whole time?
Karru marri odonna loma molonu kararo.
What language is that?
Karru marri odonna loma molonu Kararo

CLACK
Did you just blink? That's not possible!
Must be last-minute jitters.
Showtime, Kris! Time for you and Mr. Wood to kick off the show!
GULP!
Your hands are clammy!
Huh?
CLAP CLAP
You're gonna be just great!
...

Pssst!
Are you having trouble?
Hey, lady!
What time does the blimp go up?
Her face reminds me of a wart I had removed.
KRIS!
Ooh! Ooh! If we count your chins, will it tell us your age?
Kris! That's ENOUGH!
You're enough for two!
IF YOU GOT ANY BIGGER, YOU'D NEED YOUR OWN ZIP CODE!
REALLY, KRIS!!!
I'm not doing it! I'm not saying these things!
Please apologize to me and the audience!
APOLOGIZE FOR THIS!

BLAST
SPEW
SPLASH
GASP
GAH!
CLEAR THE AUDITORIUM!!!
I DON'T KNOW HOW YOU DID THAT, OR WHY...
. . . BUT I'M GOING TO SEE THAT YOU ARE SUSPENDED FOR LIFE!!!

Sickening! Totally sickening!
YOU HAVE TO LISTEN TO ME! IT WASN'T A PRACTICAL JOKE!
On Monday I'm taking that dummy back to the pawnshop!
DON'T WAIT! LET'S GO NOW! PLEASE!
You are grounded till I have a chance to even process all the crazy things you've done!
Lindy, I need at least you to believe me!
I don't know what to believe anymore.
No...please, not again...
THUMP
THUMP

PLAYTIME IS OVER, SLAVES!
But--you're just a DUMMY!
SO ARE YOU!
WHAT THE-- MR. WOOD?! HE'S ALIVE?!
THAT'S WHAT I'VE BEEN TRYING TO TELL YOU!
BUT HOW IS THAT POSSIBLE?
KRIS BROUGHT ME BACK TO LIFE! WHEN SHE READ THE ANCIENT WORDS!
What should we do?
THERE'S NOTHING YOU CAN DO!
EXCEPT OBEY MY EVERY COMMAND! MWA-HA-HA!

GOTCHA!
HOW DARE YOU!
Now what?
RELEASE ME, SERVANT!
There's a piece of paper in his right pants pocket!
HEY! THAT'S MINE!
Karru marri odonna loma molonu Kararo!
FOOLS! THOSE AREN'T THE WORDS TO KILL ME! YOU ARE WASTING YOUR BREATH!
HOLD HIM TIGHT, LINDY!
WHAT ARE YOU DOING?
If the magic words don't work, we have to try and kill him ourselves!
SUCH VIOLENCE! I COMMAND YOU TO LET GO OF MY HEAD!

It won't give. We need a backup plan!
Grab the suitcase from the closet!
Stay still, creep!
NEVER, SLAVE!
OOMF!
ZIP
I still think we should wake up Mom!
She won't believe us! Besides, I have an idea!

We took a shovel from the garage and headed to the lot next door.
You dig first then I'll take a turn.
Great plan.
I'M WARNING YOU! I HAVE POWERS!
LET ME OUT NOW AND YOUR PUNISHMENT WON'T BE TOO SEVERE!
DIG FASTER!
SHUNK
How much deeper?
YOU'LL BE SORRY!
MUCH DEEPER!
FLOOSH
Eventually...
I've never felt so tired in my life!
PLOP
I'm just so happy we got rid of that awful creature!
Hope Mom doesn't ask what happened to our suitcase.

The next day...
RUMBLE
Construction started early this morning.
≈UGH≈ Don't they know it's a Saturday?
RUMBLE
I wonder if they'll flatten that big mound of dirt. That would really be excellent.
≈SIGH≈ Time to face the music.
Looks like you got a temporary reprieve. Mom had to run an errand and won't be back till noon.
Guess she can't be too mad if she made crescent rolls.
I'M VERY UNHAPPY WITH YOU TWO SLAVES.

RUFF! RUFF! PANT!
I HAVE TO PUNISH YOU, TO PROVE THAT I'M SERIOUS.
Barky!
YOU WILL DO AS I SAY OR ONE BY ONE, THOSE YOU LOVE WILL SUFFER!
GASP! WHEEZE!
LET GO OF HIM!
I WARNED YOU! THE DOG MUST DIE NOW!
NO!
UNHAND ME, SLAVES!

WHEEZE!
YOU'LL PAY FOR THIS HUMILIATION!
What do we do with him now?
OUTSIDE!
THIS IS YOUR LAST CHANCE!
BEEP BEEP
Are you thinking what I'm thinking?

THIS IS MY FINAL WARNING!
RUMBLE
On the count of three! We'll toss him in front of that steamroller!
One...
...two...
I WILL UNLEASH MY FULL POWERS!
YIP!
SPLASH
BARKY! NO!
RUMBLE
RUMBLE

HONK HONK
YAP!
SPLASH
HEY! GET AWAY FROM HERE! ARE YOU GIRLS CRAZY?!
SLOOSH
SLURP
GASP!
GASP! OH, NO!
RUFF!
I'M FREE!!!

GET HIM!
SPLASH
SPLASH
SO LONG, SUCKERS! I'M OUTTA--
SPLOOSH
CRUNCH
What the--?!
HISSS
YUCK! It stinks!
Smells like rotten eggs!
SNIFF SNIFF

A kid? I ran over a kid?!
No, it was a ventriloquist dummy. Totally not alive.
Sorry to scare you like that.
Hey! You want this thing?
Best to throw it in the trash.
And so, we headed back to our room, reflecting on how all our troubles began.
Here's to no more competitions! Like ever?
DEAL.
Um, Lindy... Did you leave Slappy propped up like that?
Huh?

HEY, SLAVES! IS THAT OTHER GUY GONE?
I THOUGHT HE'D NEVER LEAVE!
MWA HAHAHA
THE END!